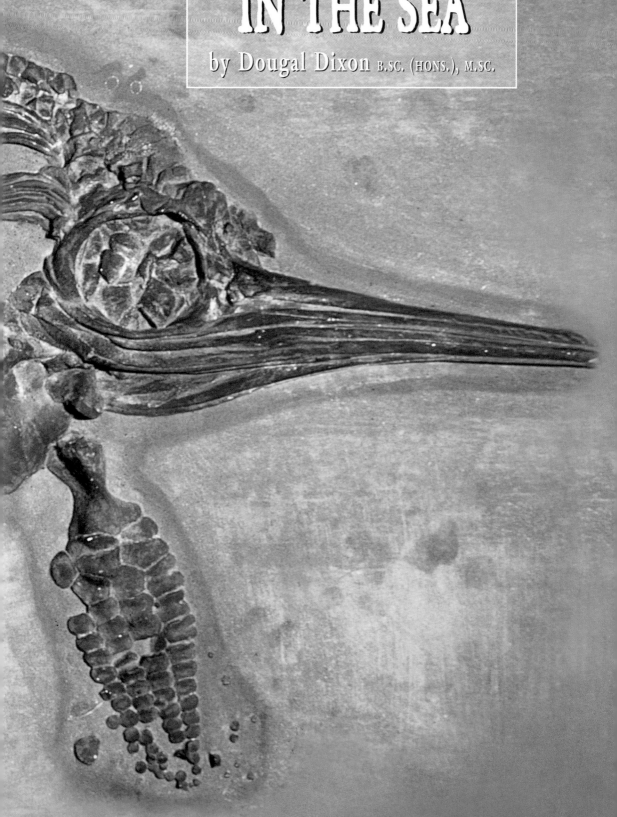

IN THE SEA

by Dougal Dixon B.SC. (HONS.), M.SC.

A RETRO-PIONEER

Spinoaequalis was the earliest-known land animal to re-adapt itself to a water-living existence. It was a lizard-like beast found in late Carboniferous marine sediments of Kansas in the United States. Its name means 'equal spine', which refers to the strong spines on the tail that made a flat vertical paddle and allowed for the attachment of strong muscles – in short, the tail of a swimming animal. The rest of the skeleton is that of a land-living creature.

A FRESHWATER PUZZLE

Mesosaurus was a freshwater reptile, about a metre (3 ft) long, with a flattened swimming tail and powerful webbed hind legs. It probably used its tail and hind legs to drive itself through the water, and steered and stabilized itself with its webbed front feet. Its teeth were fine and needle-like and were probably used for filtering invertebrates from the water to eat. The odd thing about it, though, is the fact that its skeletons are found in early Permian rocks in both South Africa and Brazil. Scientists wondered how the remains of a freshwater animal were fossilized on two widely separated continents. It was the first piece of evidence in support of a revolutionary concept called 'plate tectonics'.

THE PROOF OF DRIFT

In Permian times, when *Mesosaurus* was alive, there was no Atlantic Ocean. What is now Africa and South America were part of a single vast landmass call Pangaea. The same kinds of animal lived all over the world because there were no oceans to separate them. The presence of the skeleton of *Mesosaurus* in both South Africa and Brazil was one of the first pieces of evidence put forward to support the theory of continental drift – now better known as 'plate tectonics'.

THE FIRST SWIMMERS

All life came from the sea. It has been estimated that life appeared about 3,500 million years ago, and only relatively recently did it come out on to land (about 400 million years ago for plants and 300 million years ago for animals). Some of the first land creatures were to evolve into reptiles and the dinosaurs. But the ways of evolution are devious. Almost as soon as land life had become established, there was a tendency for a return to the sea to exploit new food sources. As early as 250 million years ago, there were water-living animals that had evidently evolved from land-living ancestors even before the dinosaurs.

A MODERN EXAMPLE

The Galapagos marine iguana looks and lives very much like some of these early swimming reptiles. It has adopted a partially aquatic way of life because it feeds on seaweed. Its lizard body, legs and feet show that it is a land-living animal, but its muscular, flexible tail is ideal for swimming. It also has the ability to hold its breath for long periods and a method for removing from its system excess salt absorbed from the seawater. These are adaptations that can never show up on fossil animals, so we do not know if early swimming reptiles had them or not.

THE BUOYANCY PROBLEM

Hovasaurus from late Permian rocks found in Madagascar had a swimming tail twice the length of the rest of its body. It was so long that it would have been difficult to use on land. However the feet were those of a land-living reptile. Most skeletons of *Hovasaurus* have pebbles lying in the stomach area. Evidently this animal swallowed stones to adjust its buoyancy underwater. This is one of the swimming techniques used by animals whose ancestors were land-living animals (*see page 10*).

CARBONIFEROUS 360-286 MYA	PERMIAN 286-245 MYA	TRIASSIC 245-208 MYA	EARLY/MID JURASSIC 208-157 MYA	LATE JURASSIC 157-146 MYA

THE CRETACEOUS SEAS

The shallow seas of the late Cretaceous period (such as those that covered central North America) were filled with ammonites. By this time the ammonites were not just the free-floating and actively hunting ammonites, but also included drifting filter-feeding forms and crawling types that fed on the seabed like giant snails. The fish-hunters of the shallow inshore waters were the mosasaurs, while out to sea lived the elasmosaurs and the giant pliosaurs. There were still pterosaurs fishing from the sky, but now they were joined by the creatures that were to be their successors – the birds.

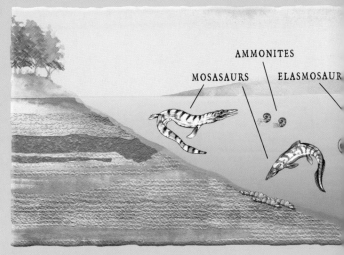

AMMONITES

MOSASAURS

ELASMOSAUR

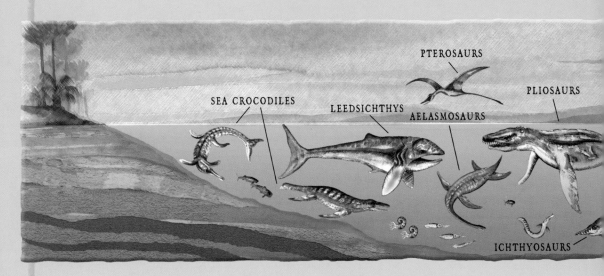

SEA CROCODILES

LEEDSICHTHYS

PTEROSAURS

AELASMOSAURS

PLIOSAURS

ICHTHYOSAURS

THE TRIASSIC SEAS

The shellfish on the shallow floor of the Triassic seas were eaten by the slow-moving placodonts. Fish were chased by the precursors of the plesiosaurs, the nothosaurs. Long-bodied ichthyosaurs also chased the fish and the ammonites (prehistoric molluscs) of the time. We are still not sure where the giant ichthyosaurs fitted into this pattern. They were probably fish-eaters and ammonite-eaters as well, and could hunt in the deep waters.

ICHTHYOSAURS

PLACODONTS

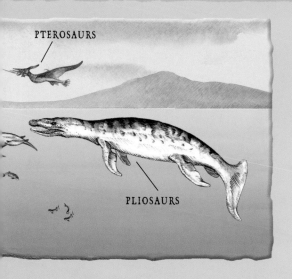

PTEROSAURS

PLIOSAURS

THE JURASSIC SEAS

The shallow seas that covered much of northern Europe in Jurassic times were bountiful, supporting many different kinds of animals. There was even a giant filter-feeding fish, *Leedsichthys*, that must have lived and fed like a modern basking shark. Inshore, in shallow waters, lived the sea crocodiles, feeding on the fish of the area. The fish and ammonites of the deeper waters were hunted by ichthyosaurs, while closer to the surface they were hunted by elasmosaurs which were, in turn, hunted by the great pliosaurs. Dipping into the waves to fish, were the flying reptiles, the pterosaurs.

NOTHOSAURS

GIANT ICHTHYOSAURS

AN ECOLOGICAL OVERVIEW

The prehistoric seas and oceans were full of life and supported complex food chains. At the bottom of the food chain were the algae, growing and reproducing by absorbing energy from the sun and taking nutrition from the water round about. Filter-feeding animals like molluscs fed on these, and in turn were preyed upon by fish and other vertebrates. Higher up the chain, these creatures were threatened by even bigger invertebrates who were themselves foodstuff for the largest and most powerful of the sea animals. When any of these animals died they decayed and the substance of their bodies went to provide nutrition in the seawater, which allowed the algae to grow. It was all an interlinked cycle.

LIFE AFTER DEATH

The science of taphonomy deals with what happens to an animal after it dies, and how it becomes a fossil. At sea this can be relatively simple.

1. When an animal dies it may float at the surface for a while until the gases generated in its decaying tissues disperse.

2. Eventually, however, it sinks to the bottom of the sea. A less buoyant animal may go straight to the bottom. There it may be scavengend by bottom-living creatures, and its parts broken up and dispersed.

3. If sand and mud are being deposited rapidly on the sea bed the body is quickly buried before too much damage is done.

4. After millions of years the sand and mud will be compressed and cemented together as rock, and the bones of the dead animal will have been replaced by minerals. It will have become a fossil.

A MODERN TURTLE

The turtle is a slow-moving aquatic reptile, shelled above and below, with paddle limbs that allow it to move through the water with a flying action. Protected from its enemies and surrounded by sources of food, it does not need speed or a streamlined shape to thrive.

AN EARLY WINNER

A broad body shape is adequate for a slow-moving animal, but such a creature remains vulnerable to attack from predators. This threat encouraged the development of armour in such reptiles. The end result was the turtle. The earliest turtle, *Proganochelys*, dates from the late Triassic period, and lived in Germany. Its body shape and the arrangement of the shell is very similar to the modern turtle, which has not evolved much in 215 million years.

BIG IS BEAUTIFUL

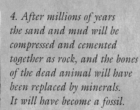

The biggest turtle known, *Archelon*, cruised the inland sea that covered much of North America in late Cretaceous times. At almost four metres (13 ft) long it was bigger than a rowing boat. Its shell was reduced to a system of bony struts covered by tough skin; much like the biggest of the modern turtles, the leatherback. It probably fed on soft things like jellyfish, as just like the modern leatherback, its jaws were not very strong.

A SHOAL OF SWIMMING REPTILES

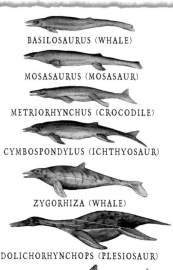

BASILOSAURUS (WHALE)

MOSASAURUS (MOSASAUR)

METRIORHYNCHUS (CROCODILE)

CYMBOSPONDYLUS (ICHTHYOSAUR)

ZYGORHIZA (WHALE)

DOLICHORHYNCHOPS (PLESIOSAUR)

BAPTANODON (ICHTHYOSAUR)

DELPHINOSAURUS (ICHTHYOSAUR)

We have a good record of water-living animals because in an environment where sediment is constantly accumulating, these creatures have a better chance of being fossilised. From these fossils, we know that many of the sea creatures were in fact reptiles that had left dry land for a new life in the water. If there was more food in the water than on land, and if there were fewer dangerous predators in the sea, an aquatic life would have become enticing. Reptiles can adapt quite easily to such a lifestyle. They have a low metabolic rate and they can cope without oxygen for some time. In addition, moving around in the water takes only about a quarter of the energy of moving about on land.

AN IDEAL SHAPE

The best shape for an underwater hunter is a streamlined body with a strong flattened tail and paddle limbs. Many of the Permian, Triassic, Jurassic and Cretaceous swimming reptiles were built like this as were the tertiary whales. Some had strange adaptations like long necks that probably enabled them to reach prey hiding in rocks.

TRIASSIC 245-208 MYA	EARLY/MID JURASSIC 208-157 MYA	LATE JURASSIC 157-146 MYA	EARLY CRETACEOUS 146-97 MYA	LATE CRETACEOUS 97-65 MYA

PLACODONTS - THE SHELL-SEEKERS

PLACODUS

The most typical of the placodonts was *Placodus* itself. In appearance it looked rather like an enormous newt, about two metres (7 ft) long, with a chunky body, a paddle-shaped tail, webbed feet and a short head.

There are all kinds of reasons why water-living animals should evolve from land-living animals. Most persuasive of these is the idea that when a good food supply exists, then nature will develop something to exploit it.

Shellfish represent one such food supply. The earliest group of reptiles that seemed to be particularly well adapted to feeding on shellfish were the placodonts. Although they still needed to come to the surface to breathe, they rooted about on the bed of the Tethys Sea that spread across southern Europe in Triassic times.

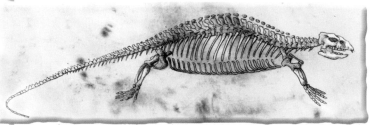

BUILT FOR BUOYANCY

A glimpse of the skeleton of *Placodus* reveals one of its main adaptations to its underwater way of life - 'pachystosis'. This means that the bones were broad and heavy, perfect for feeding on the bottom of the ocean. Animals that have pachystosis also have big lungs to help to regulate their buoyancy. To accommodate its huge lungs, *Placodus* developed a broad rib cage. A modern animal with these adaptations is the sea otter. Its weight and large lung capacity enable it to walk along the sea bed with ease, hunting shellfish. *Placodus* would have had the same lifestyle.

TRIASSIC 245-208 MYA	EARLY/MID JURASSIC 208-157 MYA	LATE JURASSIC 157-146 MYA	EARLY CRETACEOUS 146-97 MYA	LATE CRETACEOUS 97-65 MYA

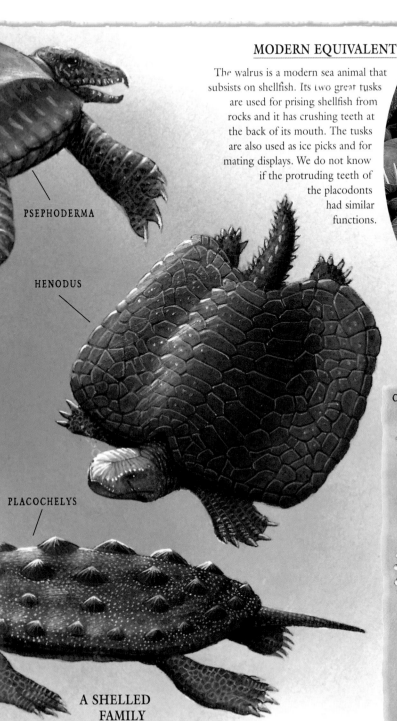

PSEPHODERMA

HENODUS

PLACOCHELYS

The walrus is a modern sea animal that subsists on shellfish. Its two great tusks are used for prising shellfish from rocks and it has crushing teeth at the back of its mouth. The tusks are also used as ice picks and for mating displays. We do not know if the protruding teeth of the placodonts had similar functions.

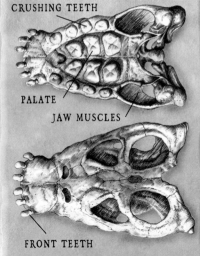

CRUSHING TEETH

PALATE

JAW MUSCLES

FRONT TEETH

POWERFUL BITE

From below, the protruding front teeth of *Placodus* are obvious. These were used for plucking the shells from the rocks and the seafloor. Further back the jaws have strong crushing teeth, and even the palate has a pavement of broad flat teeth, all ideal for smashing up the shells of shellfish. Holes in the side of the skull show where very powerful jaw muscles were attached. *Placodus* would have eaten bivalves similar to those that survive today, and brachiopods.

A SHELLED FAMILY

Because they were slow moving animals, the placodonts must have been very vulnerable to the meat-eaters of the time. Many developed shells on their backs as protection. In some types, the shells were very extensive and looked very much like those of turtles, but the two groups of animals were in no way related. The similar shells developed independently among animals that had the same lifestyle in the same environment – a process known as 'convergent evolution'.

9

DUCKBILLED PLATYPUS

The duckbilled platypus is an ancient animal with webbed feet that push the water back behind, driving the animal forward. Such a motion is quite primitive. Later marine animals had limbs that had evolved into flippers that were built like wings, allowing the animal to travel through the water in a flying motion. Nothosaurs seem to represent a halfway stage between the primitive platypus and more advanced sea creatures. Some nothosaurs had webbed feet, while some had paddles.

LARIOSAURUS

NOTHOSAURUS

A VARIETY OF NOTHOSAURS

Although the nothosaurs conformed to a particular shape, there was much variation within the group.

Nothosaurus (from which the group gets its name) was 3 metres (10 ft) long, and had a very long head with jaws full of little teeth. *Lariosaurus*, at 60 cm (24 inches) one of the smallest nothosaurs, was very primitive and looked very much like a land- living animal that happened to be swimming in the sea. Big *Ceresiosaurus*, on the other hand, had feet that were almost like paddles, and a small head on a long neck.

TRIASSIC 245-208 MYA	EARLY/MID JURASSIC 208-157 MYA	LATE JURASSIC 157-146 MYA	EARLY CRETACEOUS 146-97 MYA	LATE CRETACEOUS 97-65 MYA

BETWEEN THE LAND & THE SEA

The nothosaurs preceeded the plesiosaurs, rulers of the late Jurassic and Cretaceous seas. Like the placodonts, they are known mostly from the sediments laid down in the Tethys Sea, an ancient ocean that lay in the position where the Mediterranean Sea occupies today. Their necks, bodies and tails were long and they had webbed feet (although they could still walk on land). Their hind limbs were more massive than their front limbs and were used mostly for swimming. They had many small pointed teeth in long narrow jaws for catching fish. Nothosaurs seem to represent a part-way stage between land-living animals and fish-eating seagoing ones like the plesiosaurs.

LET'S GO FISHING

The long jaws and sharp teeth of *Nothosaurus* were ideal for catching fish. The long neck would have been able to reach fast-swimming fish quickly, and the little teeth would have held the slippery prey firmly. These teeth can be seen in modern fish-eating animals like crocodiles.

CERESIOSAURUS

NOTHOSAUR FOSSIL

Nothosaur fossils are known from the Alps and from China. Although these animals had legs and toes, their limb bones were not strongly joined to one another and the hips and shoulders were quite weak. This degenerate state shows that they were not well adapted for moving about on land and were better at swimming than walking.

STOMACH STONES

Most good fossilized skeletons of pliosaurs contain collections of gastroliths (stomach stones). Sea-living animals swallow stones to help to adjust their ballast (weight). We find this in animals that swim fast to cach their prey. It is a more versatile system than building up the weight of the skeleton through pachystosis, a method adopted by the placodonts (*see page 8*).

PLIOSAUR TOOTHMARKS

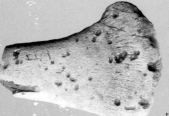

The limb bones of an elasmosaur found in late Jurassic marine rocks in Dorset, England, have given scientists a dramatic clue as to the feeding habits of the pliosaurs. Tooth marks punched deep into the bones match exactly the set of teeth of a big pliosaur. Until this discovery scientists thought that pliosaurs ate only fish and squid.

UNDERWATER ATTACK

From all this evidence we can build up a picture of a late Jurassic marine incident. A long-necked elasmosaur is feeding near the surface. A pliosaur cruises at some depth below, hunting fish and squid. Through the taste of the water it detects the presence of the other reptile. Vomiting out a few stomach stones it adjusts its buoyancy to allow it to rise. Then, when its prey is in view, it 'flies' towards it with strong thrusts of its flippers, closing in on a paddle with its mouthful of teeth. Then, having secured a firm hold, the pliosaur twists its massive body, ripping the unfortunate elasmosaur apart before eating it.

TRIASSIC	EARLY/MID JURASSIC	LATE JURASSIC	EARLY CRETACEOUS	LATE CRETACEOUS
245-208 MYA	208-157 MYA	157-146 MYA	146-97 MYA	97-65 MYA

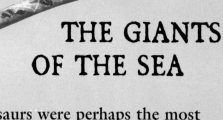

THE GIANTS OF THE SEA

The plesiosaurs were perhaps the most varied group of swimming reptiles during the time of the dinosaurs. They were ocean-going fish-eaters, ranging in size from the length of a small seal to that of a medium-sized whale. They had broad bodies, short tails and two pairs of wing-like paddles with which they flew through the ocean waters. One group had short necks and long heads, while the other had long necks and very small heads (*see pages 14–17*). The short-necked types are called the pliosaurs, and the long-necked types the elasmosaurs. The pliosaurs were the larger of the two groups – the sperm whales of the Mesozoic seas.

IN FOR THE KILL

Broad flanges at the back of the skull of a pliosaur must have held massive neck muscles. This suggests that pliosaurs grabbed their larger prey and pulled it to bits with a twisting action. Crocodiles in deep water dismember their food in exactly this way today.

BIG MOUTH

The most spectacular feature of the skeleton of a pliosaur is its huge skull. The long jaws were armed with many sharp teeth, ideal for catching big fish and squid and also for seizing larger prey. The nostrils are surprisingly small and would not have been used for breathing. Instead they would have been used for tasting the water and for judging the speed at which the animal was swimming. A pliosaur probably breathed through its mouth when it came to the surface.

A RANGE OF PLIOSAURS

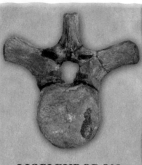

**LIOPLEURODON
VETEBRAE**

This is a vertebrae from
Liopleurodon, which
existed in northern
European waters at the
end of the Jurassic period.
Pliosaurs were a very
wide-ranging group, with
very similar animals
existing in Europe at one
time, and also at the other
side of the world in
Australia 80 million years
later. It was probably
Liopleurodon that attacked
the elasmosaur in the
incident described
on page 12.

We used to think that the pliosaurs were the
biggest sea reptiles of all time. Nowadays,
however, we are finding the remains of beasts that
were even bigger (*see page 21*). Nevertheless the biggest
of the pliosaurs were very big animals indeed.

There were also many smaller pliosaurs. Their different
sizes and head shapes reflected the different lifestyles
and the different foods that they were eating. Some
must have lived like penguins, darting and snatching at
the weaving and dispersing fish shoals, but the biggest
must have been the dolphins and toothed whales of their
time. Often all that we know of a particular pliosaur is
the skull. As all the bodies were built to a
particular well-known plan, scientists
assume that we know what the rest
of the body was like. Sometimes
that gives rise to
misconceptions.

MONSTER OF THE DEEP

We used to think that the skull of the pliosaur *Kronosaurus* represented
less than a quarter of the length of the whole animal, giving a total length
of 12-14 metres (40–46 ft) – greater than the contemporary *Tyrannosaurus* on
land. More recent studies suggest that the skull was about a third of the total
length, making it 8 metres (26 ft) long. Still quite a monster!

TRIASSIC 245-208 MYA	EARLY/MID JURASSIC 208-157 MYA	LATE JURASSIC 157-146 MYA	EARLY CRETACEOUS 146-97 MYA	LATE CRETACEOUS 97-65 MYA

A HALF-WAY STAGE

Fossilized bones of sea animals are much more common than those of land animals. They are often found on beaches, where the sea is eroding cliffs of Mesozoic (the era from the Triassic to the Cretaceous) rock, or in quarries where the right kind of rock is being extracted. One of the most complete plesiosaur skeletons ever found was five metre (16 ft) long *Rhomaleosaurus*, uncovered in 1851 from stone quarries in Barrow upon Soar, Leicestershire, central England. It was locally known as the 'Barrow Kipper' because of the appearance of its spread ribs, and has become the mascot of the village. Scientifically, the odd thing about *Rhomaleosaurus* is the fact that it has a long neck as well as a fairly large head. It is classed as a pliosaur, but it seems to be a part-way stage between the short-necked pliosaurs and the long-necked elasmosaurs.

SUPER-PENGUINS

Dolichorhynchops was a much smaller pliosaur, about three metres (10 ft) long in total. It lived in the seas that covered late Cretaceous Manitoba in Canada. Judging by its build and its teeth, it swam agilely among the shoals of fish that frequented the waters, snapping them up in its long narrow jaws. It had the same kind of swimming technique as modern penguins, using paddles to get around.

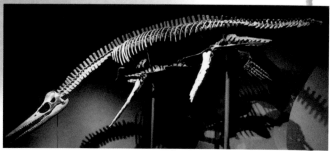

UNDERWATER FLIGHT

The plesiosaur paddle worked like a wing. Among the pliosaurs, the strongest muscles pushed the paddles forwards, so this must have been the power stroke. Among the elasmosaurs, there was as much muscle to pull the paddle back as there was to push it forward, allowing the body to turn very quickly. This suggests that the elasmosaurs had much more manoeuvrability than pliosaurs. Nowadays penguins use the same kind of swimming action.

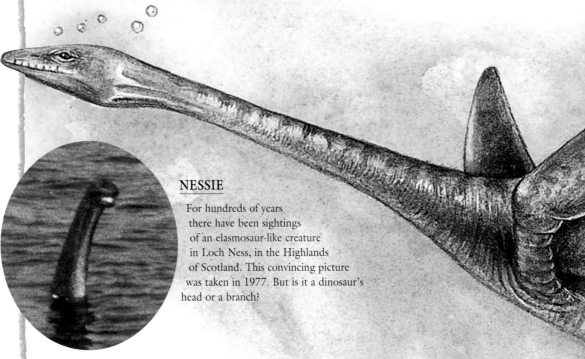

NESSIE

For hundreds of years there have been sightings of an elasmosaur-like creature in Loch Ness, in the Highlands of Scotland. This convincing picture was taken in 1977. But is it a dinosaur's head or a branch?

ARTISTIC IMPRESSIONS

Because of the numerous fossils, the remains of plesiosaurs have been known to fossil collectors for a long time before dinosaurs were discovered. This 19th century engraving of a prehistoric coastal scene depicts a giant ichthyosaur being attacked by two long-necked plesiosaurs. Although far from perfect, depictions of sea creatures were much more accurate than those of the land-living dinosaurs from the same period.

ELASMOSAURS - THE LONG-NECKS

One early researcher described the long-necked plesiosaurs as 'snakes threaded through turtles'. Indeed, the broad body and the wing-like flippers are very reminiscent of the ocean-going turtle, but the long neck and the little head full of vicious pointed teeth are very different from those of the placid grazing shelled reptile that we know today.

Elasmosaurs were the sea serpents of the time. They existed alongside the pliosaurs in the oceans of the Jurassic and Cretaceous periods.

FLEXIBILITY

The great length of the elasmosaur neck with its huge number of vertebrae have led some to suggest that it would be have been as flexible as a snake. But looking at the way the vertebrae are articulated, we can see that this was not quite true. From side to side there was quite a good degree of movement, but the neck was restricted in the up-and-down plane. Although an elasmosaur could reach downwards with ease, it could not hold its head up like a swan on the surface.

CRYPTOCLIDUS

Cryptoclidus was a common elasmosaur found in late Jurassic rocks of Europe. Its mounted skeleton can be seen in several museums. It is typical of the whole elasmosaur group, with its broad body with ribs above and below, the long neck, the mouthful of sharp outward-pointing teeth and the paddles made up of packed bone.

TRIASSIC 245-208 MYA	EARLY/MID JURASSIC 208-157 MYA	LATE JURASSIC 157-146 MYA	EARLY CRETACEOUS 146-97 MYA	LATE CRETACEOUS 97-65 MYA

ELASMOSAUR LIFESTYLE

The elasmosaurs came in all sizes. As time went on there was a tendency for the group to develop longer and longer necks. They probably hunted by ambush. The big body was probably used to disturb shoals of fish, while the little head at the end of the long neck then darted quickly into the group and speared individual fish on the long teeth. Moving the paddles in different directions would have turned the body very quickly into any direction. Their agility meant that they probably hunted on the surface as opposed to the pliosaurs, who were built for sustained cruising at great depths.

ELASMOSAURUS

We take the name of the elasmosaur group from late Cretaceous *Elasmosaurus*. This had the longest neck, in proportion to the body, of any animal known. It had 71 vertebrae, in contrast to the 28 or so sported by the earlier elasmosaurs. This neck took up more than half of the length of the entire animal.

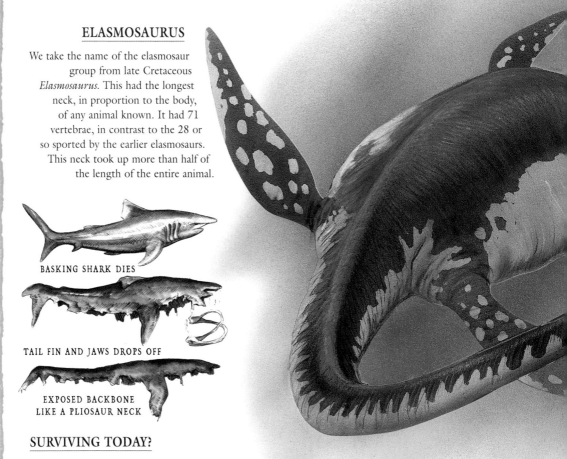

BASKING SHARK DIES

TAIL FIN AND JAWS DROPS OFF

EXPOSED BACKBONE
LIKE A PLIOSAUR NECK

SURVIVING TODAY?

Now and again we hear stories of people sighting sea serpents that have a distinct similarity to plesiosaurs. Several photographs exist of rotting carcasses with a very plesiosaur look to them. The carcasses usually turn out to be those of basking sharks. Although a basking shark looks nothing like a plesiosaur in life, its dead body deteriorates in a particular pattern. The dorsal fin and the tail fin fall off, losing the shark's distinctive profile. Then the massive jaws drop away. This leaves a tiny brain case at the end of a long string of vertebrae. Instant plesiosaur!

TRIASSIC 245-208 MYA	EARLY/MID JURASSIC 208-157 MYA	LATE JURASSIC 157-146 MYA	EARLY CRETACEOUS 146-97 MYA	LATE CRETACEOUS 97-65 MYA

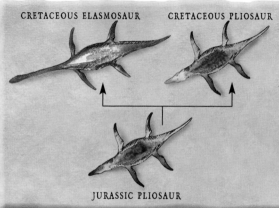

CRETACEOUS ELASMOSAUR CRETACEOUS PLIOSAUR

JURASSIC PLIOSAUR

THE 'POLYPHYLETIC' THEORY

It is possible that the elasmosaurs were 'polyphyletic' – that means that they did not evolve from the one ancestor. The Jurassic elasmosaurs evolved from the same ancestors as the nothosaurs of the Triassic period. However, the arrangement of the skull bones of the Cretaceous elasmosaurs has led some scientists to suggest that these later ones actually evolved from the short-necked pliosaurs of the Jurassic period. The long neck developed independently in response to environmental pressures – there was food to be had for long-necked animals and so long-necked animals evolved. Most scientists, however, believe that all the elasmosaurs evolved from the same ancestors – that is, they were 'monophyletic'.

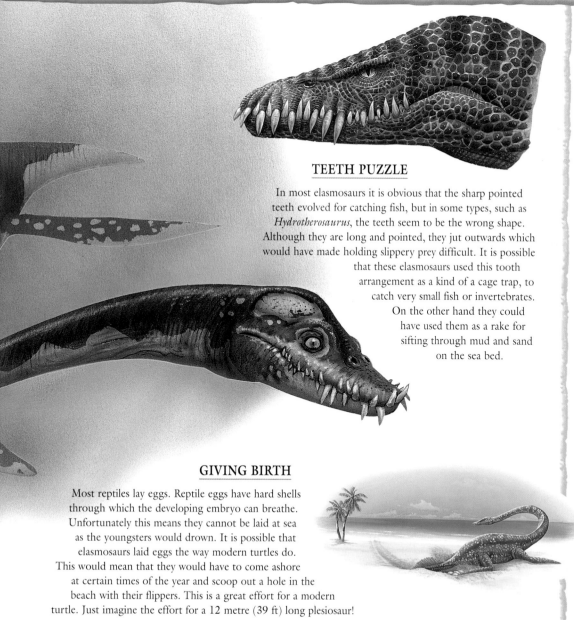

TEETH PUZZLE

In most elasmosaurs it is obvious that the sharp pointed teeth evolved for catching fish, but in some types, such as *Hydrotherosaurus*, the teeth seem to be the wrong shape. Although they are long and pointed, they jut outwards which would have made holding slippery prey difficult. It is possible that these elasmosaurs used this tooth arrangement as a kind of a cage trap, to catch very small fish or invertebrates. On the other hand they could have used them as a rake for sifting through mud and sand on the sea bed.

GIVING BIRTH

Most reptiles lay eggs. Reptile eggs have hard shells through which the developing embryo can breathe. Unfortunately this means they cannot be laid at sea as the youngsters would drown. It is possible that elasmosaurs laid eggs the way modern turtles do. This would mean that they would have to come ashore at certain times of the year and scoop out a hole in the beach with their flippers. This is a great effort for a modern turtle. Just imagine the effort for a 12 metre (39 ft) long plesiosaur!

A CLEAR IMAGE

Thinly-layered late Jurassic rocks at Holzmaden in Germany are so fine that they contain the impressions of the softest organisms that lived and died there. The bottom of the sea (where the rocks formed) was so stagnant that nothing lived – not even the bacteria that normally break down once-living matter. Among the spectacular fossils found there are the ichthyosaurs, with indications of their soft anatomy still preserved. Flesh and skin still exist as a fine film of the original carbon. For the first time it was obvious that ichthyosaurs had a dorsal fin and a big fish-like fin on the tail. We even have some indication of the colour. The carbon in the Holzmaden fossils (above) show that pigment cells were present and would have produced a dark brown tortoiseshell colour.

A MODERN RENDERING

Now it is possible to paint an accurate picture of what an ichthyosaur looked like in life. From all the fossils we have found we know that they had streamlined, dolphin-like bodies, with fins on the back and tail. Unlike dolphins the tail fin was not horizontal but vertical. There were two pairs of paddles, the front pair usually bigger than the hind pair.

THE ICHTHYOSAUR PIONEER

As with the plesiosaurs, the ichthyosaurs were known before the dinosaurs. Early naturalists, who discovered them in eroding cliffs along the Dorset coast in southern England, took them for the remains of ancient crocodiles. Indeed their long jaws and sharp teeth are very reminiscent of crocodiles. Mary Anning (1799–1847), a professional fossil collector and dealer from Lyme Regis in Dorset, is credited with finding the first complete fossil ichthyosaur when she was 12 years old. This is a myth, but her collecting and her dealings with the scientists of the day were crucial in furthering our knowledge of these creatures.

ICHTHYOSAURS - THE FISH LIZARDS

Without doubt the most well-adapted marine reptiles of the Mesozoic were the ichthyosaurs. If you saw one swimming about you might easily mistake it for a dolphin or even a shark. It is all there – the streamlined body, the triangular fin on the back, the big swimming fin on the tail and the paired swimming organs at the side. Like dolphins, ichthyosaurs were descended from land-living animals and needed to come to the surface to breathe. They evolved in Triassic times and shared the Jurassic oceans with the plesiosaurs. They did not survive far into the Cretaceous period, however, and their places were taken by another group of marine reptiles – the mosasaurs (*see pages 24–25*) – which lasted right up until the end of the Mesozoic.

ICHTHYOSAUR SKELETON

Entire skeletons of ichthyosaurs are relatively common, as these creatures were frequently fossilized. Many museums have complete ichthyosaur skeletons on display. This ichthyosaur is in the Bristol City Museum in England.

TRIASSIC 245-208 MYA	EARLY/MID JURASSIC 208-157 MYA	LATE JURASSIC 157-146 MYA	EARLY CRETACEOUS 146-97 MYA	LATE CRETACEOUS 97-65 MYA

A RANGE OF ICHTHYOSAURS

Before the standard dolphin shape of the ichthyosaur evolved, there were all different shapes and sizes, particularly among the earlier ichthyosaurs in the Triassic seas. These different types all had different lifestyles and swimming techniques. Some were long and narrow like eels, without a significant tail fin. These probably swam with a flying motion, like the plesiosaurs and penguins, and steered with their long tails. Some were the size of whales, with increased bone mass to make them heavier and able to swim in deep waters for long periods. This wide range of Triassic forms soon settled to the classic dolphin shape of the Jurassic ichthyosaur.

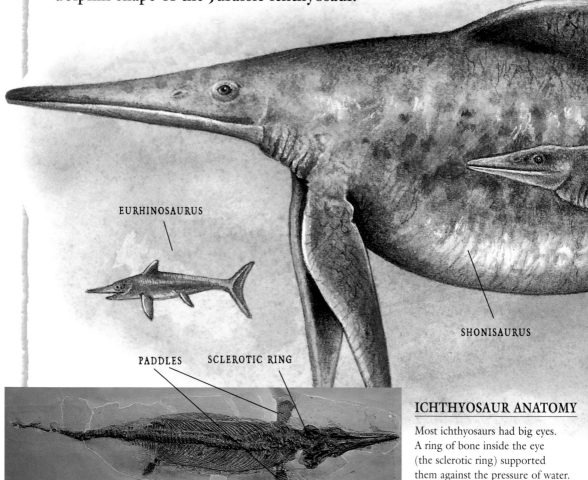

EURHINOSAURUS

SHONISAURUS

PADDLES   SCLEROTIC RING

ICHTHYOSAUR ANATOMY

Most ichthyosaurs had big eyes. A ring of bone inside the eye (the sclerotic ring) supported them against the pressure of water. Like the plesiosaurs they showed hyperphalangy (an increase in the number of joints in the finger), but they also showed hyperdactyly (an increase in the number of fingers themselves). This increased the rigidity of the paddles, which were solid pavements of bone.

SWIMMING

TAIL

PADDLES

An ichthyosaur's swimming motion (at least that of the dolphin-shaped ichthyosaurs) depended on the complex interaction of thrust and the centre of balance. The tail gave a forward and upward thrust directed through the centre of balance, and the paddles adjusted the trim. Curving itself in a vertical plane, the ichthyosaur could dive and surface. The easiest way of turning would be to execute this movement and use its paddles to roll itself on to its side.

TRIASSIC GIANT

A truly enormous Triassic ichthyosaur was discovered in British Columbia, Canada, in 1998. At 23 metres (75 ft) long it was longer than a sperm whale and approached the length of most blue whales. The skeleton is 30 per cent longer than any other marine reptile so far discovered, and its head is 5.8 metres (19 ft) long. It is still being studied and does not yet have a name.

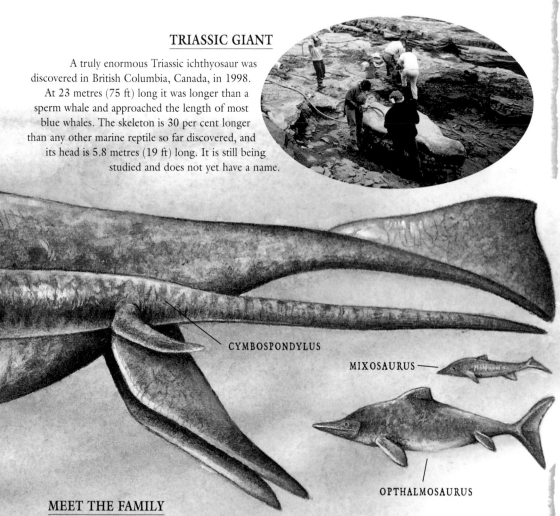

CYMBOSPONDYLUS

MIXOSAURUS

OPTHALMOSAURUS

MEET THE FAMILY

Probably the most primitive-looking ichthyosaur was *Cymbospondylus*, found in the middle Triassic rocks of Nevada in the United States. At 10 metres (33 ft) long it was a big animal, but its body was long and eel-like. *Mixosaurus* from middle Triassic rocks from all around the world was still long and slim, but it showed the beginnings of the typical ichthyosaur tail. The 15-metre (49 ft) monster *Shonisaurus* from the late Triassic rocks of Nevada was the biggest ichthyosaur known before the discovery of the Canadian giant (*see above*). *Opthalmosaurus* was probably the most fish-like and had no teeth in its jaws. It may have fed on soft-bodied animals like squid. *Eurhinosaurus* had a swordfish-like beak on its upper jaw, possibly used for stunning fish prey.

TRIASSIC 245-208 MYA	EARLY/MID JURASSIC 208-157 MYA	LATE JURASSIC 157-146 MYA	EARLY CRETACEOUS 146-97 MYA	LATE CRETACEOUS 97-65 MYA

ICHTHYOSAURS -
DISPELLING A MYTH

Reptiles lay eggs on land – that is what distinguishes them from their ancestors the amphibians. However, occasionally, reptiles that live in very harsh environments in which exposed eggs would be vulnerable tend to give birth to live young. Most of the modern reptiles that live in northern Europe bear live young – such as the common lizard, the slow worm and the adder. The ichthyosaurs also did this.

WHAT'S FOR DINNER?

The fossils of baby ichthyosaurs found inside the skeletons of the adults once led people to think that ichthyosaurs were cannibalistic. Now we know that this could not have been so as the young were located a long way from the stomach area, the little skeletons were complete and not chewed up and they were facing forwards, not backwards as they would have been if they had been swallowed.

HOLZMADEN

In late Jurassic times, a shallow sea with scattered islands covered most of northern Europe. To the north was low-lying land, and to the south, beyond a series of massive reefs formed by corals and sponges, lay the open ocean. The region of Holzmaden may have been a seasonal gathering place for ichthyosaurs where they came to give birth. We can tell much about the ichthyosaurs' anatomy and lifestyle from such fossils found in the region. A large number of ichthyosaur remains show baby ichthyosaurs emerging from the adult. These tell us that ichthyosaur birth was a very traumatic event that sometimes proved fatal for the mother.

TRIASSIC 245-208 MYA	EARLY/MID JURASSIC 208-157 MYA	LATE JURASSIC 157-146 MYA	EARLY CRETACEOUS 146-97 MYA	LATE CRETACEOUS 97-65 MYA

LITTLE ONES

This ichthyosaur from Holzmaden in Germany has been preserved with the broken-up skeletons of unborn young still intact. A fourth may just have been born – its skeleton can be seen below the tail of the parent. The mother must have given birth underwater and died in the process.

TAIL

BABY ICHTHYOSAURS

FISH FOOD

Belemnites were squid-like animals that swarmed in the warm shallow seas of the Jurassic period. Like squid they had tentacles that were armed with tiny hooks, but unlike squid their bodies were stiffened with bullet-shaped internal shells. These shells are commonly found as fossils in Jurassic rocks. We know that many ichthyosaurs ate belemnites, because we have found masses of their indigestible hooks in the stomach areas of ichthyosaur fossils.

A SWIMMING LIZARD

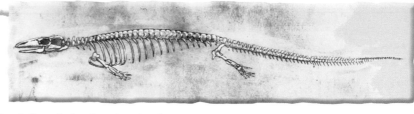

The aigalosaurs were ancesters of the mosasaurs. They were a group of swimming lizards from the late Jurassic and early to middle Cretaceous periods that lived in Europe. They grew up to a metre long, and had flattened tails but lacked the specialized paddle limbs of their descendants.

DINNER TIME

There is direct evidence that mosasaurs ate the abundant ammonites of the time. The ammonites were relatives of the modern squid and nautilus, and sported coiled shells that are very common as fossils. They lived throughout the Mesozoic in the seas all over the world. One ammonite fossil has been found punctured by toothmarks that exactly match those of a small mosasaur. Evidently the reptile had to bite the ammonite sixteen times before crushing the shell and reaching the animal.

FAMILY MEMBER?

The bones of *Mosasaurus* were very similar to those of the modern monitor lizard. Despite extinction of individual species, the same lines of animals were continuing to develop into other forms. The concept of evolution that would explain such phenomena had not been developed when *Mosasaurus* was first studied.

GEORGES CUVIER

The jawbones of a completely unknown giant reptile unearthed from the underground quarries near the River Meuse convinced the French anatomist Baron Georges Cuvier (1769–1832) that there were once animals living on the Earth that were completely unlike modern types, and that these ancient animals were periodically wiped out by extinction events.

TRIASSIC 245-208 MYA	EARLY/MID JURASSIC 208-157 MYA	LATE JURASSIC 157-146 MYA	EARLY CRETACEOUS 146-97 MYA	LATE CRETACEOUS 97-65 MYA

MOSASAURS

In 1770, workmen in a chalk quarry near Maastricht in Holland uncovered a long-jawed, toothy skull. Immediately the owner of the land sued for possession – a circumstance that is all too common in the field of palaeontology even today. Then, in 1794, the French army invaded. Despite the owner's attempt to hide the skull in a cave, it was seized as booty (with the help of a bribe of 600 bottles of wine) and taken back to Paris where it was studied by legendary French anatomist Baron Cuvier. By this time it had been identified as the skull of a huge reptile related to the modern monitor lizards. British geologist William Conybeare gave it the name *Mosasaurus* ('lizard from the Meuse').

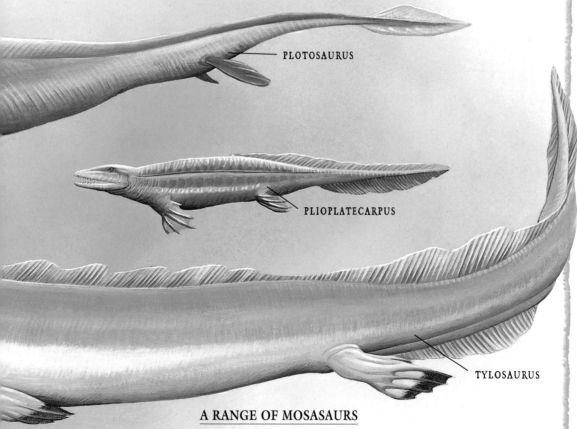

PLOTOSAURUS

PLIOPLATECARPUS

TYLOSAURUS

A RANGE OF MOSASAURS

Mosasaurs are known from late Cretaceous deposits throughout the world. They were all based on a similar body plan and ranged in size from a few metres to monsters ten metres (33 ft) or more in length. Their heads were all very similar to those of the modern monitor lizard and their teeth had adapted to snatch at fish or ammonites. An exception was *Globidens*, which had flattened rounded teeth, which were obviously adapted for a shellfish diet.

CROCODILES

Crocodiles have remained essentially unaltered since late Triassic times. However, throughout their history there have been all kinds of specialist types. Some were long-legged and scampered about on land, while some ran about on hind legs like little versions of their relatives, the dinosaurs. More significantly, some developed into sea-living forms showing the same adaptations as other sea-living reptiles – the sinuous bodies, the paddle legs and the finned tails. These were particularly important in Jurassic times.

TELEOSAURUS

METRIORHYNCHUS

GEOSAURUS

A SELECTION OF SEA CROCS

Teleosaurus was a gharial-like sea crocodile. If anything it was even longer and slimmer in build than *Steneosaurus*. *Metriorhynchus* was three metres (10 ft) long and shows much more extreme adaptations to a seagoing way of life. It lacked the armoured scales that we see on more conventional crocodiles. Its legs were converted into paddles that would have been almost useless on land. At the end of its tail the vertebral column was turned downwards, showing that it had a swimming fin like an ichthyosaur. This was a true sea crocodile. *Geosaurus* had the same adaptations as *Metriorhynchus* but appeared somewhat later and, at two metres (7 ft) long, was considerably smaller. It was much slimmer and the jaws were even narrower.

CHAMPSOSAUR

PHYTOSAUR

CROCODILE

A GOOD SHAPE

Many semi-aquatic meat-eating reptiles have crocodile shapes. The phytosaurs from the late Triassic period could be mistaken for crocodiles except for their nostrils, which were close to the eyes instead of at the tip of the snout. The champsosaurs from the late Cretaceous period of North America were also very crocodile-like, having the same lifestyle in the same habitat. None of these animals was closely related to another. This is an example of 'parallel evolution' (*see page 32*).

LIKE TODAY'S?

Looking at *Deinosuchus* from a distance you would think it was a modern crocodile. Indeed it belonged to the same family as modern crocodiles, although it lived in the late Cretaceous period. But then you notice its size – 15 metres (49 ft) long! This monster ate dinosaurs!

STENEOSAURUS

The fine shales that preserved the ichthyosaurs in the Holzmaden quarries were also very successful in preserving the marine crocodile *Steneosaurus*. We can see that it was very much like a modern crocodile. Its legs and feet show it to have been an animal that spent much of its time on land. However the occurrence of its fossils at Holzmaden and in marine deposits in England show that it was also a sea-going beast. The position of its eyes (on the top of its head) suggests that it attacked shoals of fish from below.

MODERN GHARIAL

In life *Steneosaurus* must have looked very much like the modern gharial of the Indian rivers – the same long narrow jaws with the many sharp fish-catching teeth, the same long body and tail and the same short legs. However the gharial is a river animal, while *Steneosaurus* hunted in the sea.

TRIASSIC	EARLY/MID JURASSIC	LATE JURASSIC	EARLY CRETACEOUS	LATE CRETACEOUS
245-208 MYA	208-157 MYA	157-146 MYA	146-97 MYA	97-65 MYA

AMBULOCETUS

The most primitive whale that we know was an amphibious animal. *Ambulocetus* was a kind of a halfway stage between land life and sea life. It had feet that could be used either for walking on land or swimming in the sea. To look at it would have resembled a sea lion, except that its head was long and its jaws narrow. Despite the appearance of the rest of the body, the skull of *Ambulocetus* shows it to have been a whale. It lived in the ocean area that existed between India and Asia before the Earth's plates collided, pushing the Himalayas out of the ocean.

AN EARLY WHALE

Although it sounds like a dinosaur and looks like a sea serpent, *Basilosaurus* was an early whale. With its long thin body and its sharp fish-catching teeth, it was the successor to the great mosasaurs that had become extinct just a few million years previously. At a length of 20 metres (66 ft) these were very long animals, approaching the length of today's whales, but they did not have the modern whale's great bulk.

WHAT CAME NEXT?

The great extinction event at the end of the Cretaceous period that wiped the dinosaurs and the other big land-living animals had an even greater effect on the sea. A vast number of the invertebrates (including the ammonites and the belemnites) disappeared, and with them went the big reptiles. The placodonts and the ichthyosaurs had already died out, but suddenly the elasmosaurs, the pliosaurs and the mosasaurs disappeared too, as well as the pterosaurs that winged their way overhead. This left the oceans wide open to be repopulated by something else – the mammals.

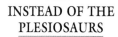

INSTEAD OF THE PLESIOSAURS

Sea lions today take the place of plesiosaurs, actively chasing fish using the flying movements of their flippers. An even closer analogy would be the replacement of the ichthyosaurs by the dolphins – even their shapes are the same.

A TEMPORARY MEASURE

About halfway through the age of mammals a peculiar group of sea mammals cropped up. Called the desmostylians, they were as big as horses. They had strange stumpy inward-turned feet which they probably used for walking across the seabed like a hippopotamus. Their teeth consisted of a bunch of forward-pointing tusks forming a kind of a shovel structure. These were probably used for grazing seaweed or even plucking shellfish, and crushing teeth at the back of the jaws would have been suitable for either. The desmostylians were a short-lived group and died out without leaving any descendants. We cannot really compare them with anything that is alive today.

LATE JURASSIC 157-146 MYA	EARLY CRETACEOUS 146-97 MYA	LATE CRETACEOUS 97-65 MYA	PALEOGENE 65-23 MYA	NEOGENE 23-2 MYA

DID YOU KNOW?

That similar looking animals can be entirely unrelated to one another?
This is known as 'convergent evolution'.
There seem to be particular shapes that fit an animal for a particular way of life in a particular environment, and these shapes crop up again and again in different animals. The classic example is the similarity in shape between the ichthyosaurs, the dolphins and the sharks – although these creatures are similar in appearance, one is a reptile, one a mammal and one a fish.

'Parallel evolution' is a similar concept.
Here, similar looking animals have developed along different routes from the same ancestors. We see this among freshwater semi-aquatic animals. Crocodiles, phytosaurs and chasmosaurs all have the same shape but they evolved quite separately from the same group of ancestral reptiles.

That there are different ways for water animals to adjust their buoyancy? Deep divers – whales, seals and ichthyosaurs – have heavy bodies and small lungs, while animals that walk on the the seabed – dugongs, desmostylans and placodonts – have heavy bones and big lungs. Those that 'fly' underwater – sea lions, penguins and plesiosaurs – swallow stones to adjust their buoyancy.

That there are bigger sea animals now than at any time in the past?
The blue whale, at 30 metres long, is far larger than any extinct sea animal that we know. The biggest giant squid that has been measured is 20 metres long, but there is ample evidence to suggest that there are even bigger ones existing in the depths that have never been seen by science. There is nothing in the fossil record to top this.

ACKNOWLEDGEMENTS

We would like to thank: Advocate, Helen Wire, www.fossilfinds.com and Elizabeth Wiggans for their assistance. Illustrations by John Alston, Lisa Alderson, Simon Mendez, Bob Nicholls and Luis Rey.
Copyright © 2003 *ticktock* Entertainment Ltd.
First published in Great Britain by ticktock Publishing Ltd., Unit 2, Orchard Business Centre, North Farm Road, Tunbridge Wells, Kent TN2 3XF.
All rights reserved.
No part of this publication may be reproduced, stored in a retrieval system, or transmitted in any form or by any means electronic, mechanical, photocopying, recording or otherwise, without prior written permission of the copyright owner.
A CIP catalogue record for this book is available from the British Library. ISBN 1 86007 234 8 (paperback). ISBN 1 86007 238 0 (hardback).

Picture Credits:
t=top, b=bottom, c=centre, l=left, r=right, OFC=outside front cover, IFC=inside front cover, IBC=inside back cover, OBC=outside back cover

University of Toronto: 2tr. Lisa Alderson: 3b, 6-7c, 15t, 16-17c, 22-23c, 28c. John Alston: 2b, 6l, 7r, 8b, 9r, 11t, 16t, 18l, 19t, 23t, 24cl, 24b, 26t. BBC Natural History Unit: 3tr, 9t, 10tl, 13cr, 26c, 29b. Corbis: 11b, 26bl. Steve Etches: 12tl. Fossil Finds: 6b, 20t, 26cl. Simon Mendez: 2c, 8-9c, 10-11c, 14-15c, 19cr, 19br, 24c & OFC, 26-27c, 28bl, 30-31c. Natural History Museum: 14tl, 17tr, 22b, 25t, 29br, 30cl. Bob Nicholls: 12-13c. Luis Rey: 8t, 18-19c, 30-32c, 28-29c, 30tl. Peterborough Museum: 13b. Royal Tyrell Museum: 23cr. Science Photo Library: 16b. University of Bristol: 21b.

Every effort has been made to trace the copyright holders and we apologize in advance for any unintentional omissions.
We would be pleased to insert the appropriate acknowledgement in any subsequent edition of this publication.

snapping-turtle
guide